San Mateo Public Library
San Mateo, CA   94402
"Questions Answered"

THE BRAZILLER SERIES OF POETRY
Richard Howard, General Editor

By Charles Simic

What the Grass Says (KAYAK PRESS)   *1967*

Somewhere Among Us A Stone Is
   Taking Notes (KAYAK PRESS)   *1969*

Dismantling the Silence (BRAZILLER)   *1971*

White (NEW RIVERS PRESS)   *1972*

Return to a Place Lit by a Glass of Milk (BRAZILLER)   *1974*

Biography and a Lament (BARTHOLOMEW'S
   COBBLE)   *1976*

TRANSLATIONS

Fire Gardens *by I. Lalic* (TRANSLATION IN COLLABO-
   RATION WITH C. W. TRUESDALE)   *1970*

The Little Box *by V. Popa*   *1970*

Four Modern Yugoslav Poets
   by I. Lalic, B. Miljkovic, L. Simovic, M. Pavic   *1970*

ANTHOLOGY

Another Republic (CO-EDITED WITH MARK STRAND,
   THE ECCO PRESS)   *1976*

CHARON'S
COSMOLOGY

CHARON'S COSMOLOGY

Poems by

CHARLES SIMIC

GEORGE BRAZILLER

New York

Some of these poems have previously appeared in the following
periodicals to whose editors grateful acknowledgment is made:
*Field, Pocket Pal, Fire Exit, Paris Review, Kayak, American
Poetry Review, Ironwood, Antioch Review, Chicago Review,
Antaeus, Marylin, Sun, The Iowa Review, New Letters.*

For information address the publisher:
George Braziller, Inc.
One Park Avenue, New York 10016

Library of Congress Cataloging in Publication Data
Simic, Charles, 1938–
Charon's cosmology.
(The Braziller series of poetry)
I. Title.
PS3569.I4725C5   811'.5'4   76-55133
ISBN 0-8076-0842-4
ISBN 0-8076-0843-2 pbk.

First Printing
Printed in the United States of America

To Nicki and Philip

Contents

I

II

I

THE PARTIAL EXPLANATION

Seems like a long time
Since the waiter took my order.
Grimy little luncheonette,
The snow falling outside.

Seems like it has grown darker
Since I last heard the kitchen door
Behind my back
Since I last noticed
Anyone pass on the street.

A glass of ice water
Keeps me company
At this table I chose myself
Upon entering.

And a longing,
Incredible longing
To eavesdrop
On the conversation
Of cooks.

AUCTION

The face of a man who can't find a job.
The sky—that ear and eye hospital.
And the streets with their pawnshops, groceries, poolhalls,
And the streets at each other's throats.

We have one bloody emaciated half-human
Ironing board to sell. We have a skeleton
Of a baby carriage. We have a ringing alarm clock without
                                        hands or numerals,
And a soul, if the devil can still find it.

It's late. Here comes Mrs. Novak who scrubs
Floors for a living. Here come two female saints
From the altar of the Mulberry Street church.
Here comes the landlord chewing on a gold toothpick.

The face of so and so who can't find a job.
The sky—that pinball machine slightly tilted . . .
And of course, right now in some cellar
They are working over a poor guy who's got nothing to confess.

A LANDSCAPE WITH CRUTCHES

So many crutches. Now even the daylight
Needs one, even the smoke
As it goes up. And the shacks—
One per customer—they move off
In a single file with difficulty,

I said, with a hell of an effort . . .
And the trees behind them about to stumble,
And the ants on their toy-crutches,
And the wind on its ghost-crutch.

I can't get any peace around here:
The bread on its artificial limbs,
A headless doll in a wheelchair,
And my mother, mind you, using
Two knives for crutches as she squats to pee.

THE VARIANT

A police dog eating grass
On a coroner's leash
Along the perimeter
Of barbed wire.

His impeccable table manners
And the evening's capacity
For lofty detachment
From the extraordinary event.

The grass like a prophet's beard,
Thoughtful and greying. Chill
Of late autumn in the air.
Distant guard-towers with searchlights
Following us all
With malice, regret,
And also absent-mindedly.

The proverbial dry blades
Sticking in the throat.

Obviously, what the poor mutt needs
Is some old stern stepmother
To tap him on the back
Quickly
Not caring to hold on.

THE ELDERS

I go to great troubles.
Bareheaded,
I visit them first thing in the morning.
Their gloomy servant ushers me in.
I, the poor cousin—
They, my benefactors
Standing with their stove-pipe hats
In a circle of splendid bloodhounds,
In a circle of sharp-nosed women.

The rain is pouring down, the rain . . .
Inside, their steps are slow, arthritic.
A slight greeting and I'm shown into the corner
Where I sit watching their pale hands,
Their hands with many tiny blue veins,
With many long and sharp fingernails,
While the curtains billow and billow
As if birds, as if large birds were caught in them.

Sights that make everyone sigh,
Except for me, interested as I am
Only in their beautiful daughter
Who touched me on the way in
With the same finger
That will loosen the button above her breasts,
In the evening
When the lights are low.

POEM

My father writes all day, all night:
Writes while he sleeps, writes in his coffin.
It's nice and quiet in our house.
You can see the specks of dust in the sunlight.

I look at times over his shoulders
At all that whiteness. The snow is falling,
As you'd expect. A drop of ink
Gets buried easily, like a footprint.

I, too, would get lost but there's his shadow
On the wall, like a perched owl.
There's the sound of his pen
And the bottle on the table sunk in thought.

When the bottle empties,
His great dark hand
Bigger than the earth
Feels for the moon's spigot.

THE SUMMONS

The robes of the judges are magnificent
When they enter among the assembled
The one with a head of a lamb will be mine,
With a throat of a lamb

Recently slit. The one all covered with burrs
Who rests his cheekbone against my summons,
Who has stubble sticking out of his ears,
The one already half-salted, half-roasted,

Who presides in this vast courtroom—
Ramshackle, gutted. A little snow beginning to fall
                              through the cracks.
Stretches of emptiness over which we
Address each other, in which we proclaim

Our identical innocence. In the gloom
Of a winter morning—black snowflakes.
The old cleaning women who sweep them
And know each one by its suffering and name.

NURSERY RHYME

The little pig goes to market.
Historical necessity. I like to recite
And you prefer to write on the blackboard.
Leap frog and marbles.

Their heads are big and their noses are short.
Lovely afternoon. The prison guards.
A street maimed so it can go on begging.
Eternal recurrence and its rubble.

Follow your calling, we follow ours.
The soldier's hand is gentle. The meadow.
People who snore have happy dreams.
Our father loves all his creatures equally.

A pig with gold teeth, says the barber.
Banks of a stream lined with willows.
Now someone's kicking him to hurry up.
Rope, a little milk for the rope.

Give me another cigarette quickly.
Misery. Its wedding photograph.
I see a blur, a speck, meagre, receding
Our lives trailing in its wake.

SONG

In her widow's purse
My mother carries
A thought heavier
Than her heart

When no one's looking
She takes it out
And chews on it
As on a crust of stale bread

When no one's looking
She sits and spits
Its bones and coals into a heap
To tuck us all in

Only its familiar weight
Will make us fall asleep

Only its maternal dark
Will make our dreams luminous

HELP WANTED

They ask for a knife
I come running
They need a lamb
I introduce myself as the lamb

A thousand sincere apologies
It seems they require some rat-poison
They require a shepherd
For their flock of black widows

Luckily I've brought my bloody
Letters of recommendation
I've brought my death certificate
Signed and notarized

But they've changed their minds again
Now they want a song-bird a bit of springtime
They want a woman
To soap and kiss their balls

It's one of my many talents
(I assure them)
Chirping and whistling like an aviary
Spreading the cheeks of my ass

ANIMAL ACTS

A bear who eats with a silver spoon.
Two apes adept at grave-digging.
Rats who do calculus.
A police dog who copulates with a woman,
Who takes undertaker's measurements.

A bedbug who suffers, who has doubts
About his existence. The miraculous
Laughing dove. A thousand-year-old turtle
Playing billiards. A chicken who
Cuts his own throat, who bleeds.

The trainer with his sugar-cubes,
With his chair and whip. The evenings
When they all huddle in a cage,
Smoking cheap cigars, lazily
Marking the cards in the new deck.

CHARON'S COSMOLOGY

With only his feeble lantern
To tell him where he is
And every time a mountain
Of fresh corpses to load up

Take them to the other side
Where there are plenty more
I'd say by now he must be confused
As to which side is which

I'd say it doesn't matter
No one complains he's got
Their pockets to go through
In one a crust of bread in another a sausage

Once in a long while a mirror
Or a book which he throws
Overboard into the dark river
Swift cold and deep

PROGRESS REPORT

And how are the rats doing in the maze?
The big fat one with baggy pants
Appears confused. You shout.
You tell him to keep running.

A pretty girl's got him by the tail.
Now she's going to dissect him.
The instruments glitter and the beads
Of perspiration on her forehead.

The others are still in the maze.
They study the stars, defecate,
Do the tango, make valentines,
Salute the general, wear mourning bands.

Her long fingers find no resistance,
Already she's got his heart open . . .
I don't know who this girl is?
Neither does he, the spellbound one.

DESCRIPTION

That which brings it
about. The agent.

The old sweet temptation
to find an equivalent

for the ineffable.
This street. Grey day

breaking. So many things
to evoke, name.

Standing here, partaking
of that necessity.

*

Among all the images
that come to mind,

where to begin?
Contortions, infinite shapes

pain assumes. Some old woman,
for instance,

a lame child
passing me by

with incredible exertions
for each step.

*

A street that always
somehow resembles me.

Grey day and I
the source of light.

A corner where
a part of myself

keeps an appointment
with another part of myself.

This small world
This dumb show.

*

The two of them,
all haunched up, limping,

hand in hand,
afraid to cross the street

on some millennial errand
to a prison, some infirmary

where they'll take bread
out of their mouths,

where a doctor
won't use any anaesthetic.

THE LESSON

It occurs to me now
that all these years
I have been
the idiot pupil
of a practical joker.

Diligently
and with foolish reverence
I wrote down
what I took to be
his wise pronouncements
concerning
my life on earth.
Like a parrot
I rattled off the dates
of wars and revolutions.
I rejoiced
at the death of my tormentors
I even became convinced
that their number
was diminishing.

It seemed to me
that gradually
my teacher was revealing to me
a pattern,
that what I was being told
was an intricate plot
of a picaresque novel
in installments,
the last pages of which
would be given over

entirely
to lyrical evocations
of nature.

Unfortunately,
with time,
I began to detect in myself
an inability
to forget even
the most trivial detail.
I lingered more and more
over the beginnings:
The haircut of a soldier
who was urinating
against our fence;
shadows of trees on the ceiling,
the day
my mother and I
had nothing to eat . . .

Somehow,
I couldn't get past
that prison train
that kept waking me up
every night.
I couldn't get that whistle
that rumble
out of my head . . .

In this classroom
austerely furnished
by my insomnia,

at the desk consisting
of my two knees,
for the first time
in this long and terrifying
apprenticeship,
I burst out laughing.
Forgive me, all of you!
At the memory of my uncle
charging a barricade
with a homemade bomb,
I burst out laughing.

HAPPY END

And then they pressed the melon
And heard it crack
And then they ate enough to burst
And then the bird sung oh so sweetly
While they sat scratching without malice
Good I said for just then
The cripples started dancing on the table
The night I met a kind of angel
Do you have a match she said
As I was unzipping her dress
Already there were plenty of them
Who had ascended to the ceiling
Lovers they were called and they held
Roses between their teeth while the Spring
Went on outside the wide open windows
And even a stick used in childbeating
Blossomed by a little crooked road
My hunch told me to follow

II

THE BALLAD OF THE WHEEL

so that's what it's like to be a wheel
so that's what it's like to be tied to one of its spokes
while the rim screeches while the hub grinds
so that's what it's like to have the earth and heaven confused
to speak of the stars on the road
of stones churning in the icy sky
to suffer as the wheel suffers
to bear its unimaginable weight

if only it were a honing wheel
I would have its sparks to see by
if only it were a mill stone
I would have bread to keep my mouth busy
if only it were a roulette wheel
my left eye would watch its right dance in it

so that's what it's like
to be chained to the wounded rib of a wheel
to move as the hearse moves
to move as the lumber truck moves
down the mountains at night

*

what do you think my love
while the wheel turns

I think of the horse out in front
how the snowflakes are caught in his mane
how he shakes his beautiful blindfolded head
I think how in the springtime
two birds are pulling us along as they fly
how one bird is a crow

and the other a swallow
I think how in the summertime
there's no one out there
except the clouds in the blue sky
except the dusk in the blue sky
I think how in autumn
there's a man harnessed out there
a bearded man with the bit stuck in his mouth
a hunchback with a blanket over his shoulders
hauling the wheel
heavy as the earth

*

don't you hear I say don't you hear
the wheel talk as it turns

I have the impression that it's hugging me closer
that it has maternal instincts
that it's telling me a bedtime story
that it knows the way home
that I grit my teeth just like my father

I have the impression
that it whispers to me
how all I have to do
to stop its turning
is to hold my breath

UNINTELLIGIBLE TERMS

A child crying in the night
Across the street
In one of the many dark windows.
A sound to get used to,
Incorporate into your routine, supposedly,
Like this textbook of astronomy
Which you study with equal apprehension
Oblique to the light of the lamp
And your shadow on the wall.
A sleepless witness at the base
Of this expanding immensity,
Simultaneous, oh God,
With all the empty spaces.
Listening to a child crying in the night
On a chance, the remote chance,
It will hush.

A WALL

That's the only image
That turns up.

A wall, all by itself,
Poorly lit, beckoning,
But no sense of the room,
Not even a hint
Of why it is I remember
That fragment so clearly:

The fly I was watching,
The details of its wings
Glowing like turquoise,
Its feet, to my amusement
Following a minute crack—
An eternity
Around that simple event.

And nothing else, and nowhere
To go back to,
And no one else
As far as I know to verify.

DEAD LETTER OFFICE

That must be where the wind
Hones its chill.
That grey building in the fog,
Its roof covered with snow.
Dream penitentiary
Without doors or windows,
Yet each dawn they add
Another dark wing to its beak.

*

They add my letter and your
Telegram. They force them
Through the cracks in the wall.
No one knows what goes on inside.
For three days I walked
Along its deserted colonnade
Without reaching the corner.
Then I lay down to rest,
One ear against its immensity.

*

You were already there.
Disguised as an employee.
Endless space
Love, and you
On your hands and knees
In the dark
Pressing
Every dead letter to your heart.

ERASER

A summons because the marvelous prey is fleeing
Something to rub out the woods
From the blackboard sound of wind and rain
A device to recover a state of pure expectancy

Only the rubbings only the endless patience
As the clearing appears the clearing which is there
Without my even having to look
The domain of the marvelous prey

This emptiness which gets larger and larger
As the eraser works and wears out
As my mother shakes her apron full of little erasers
For me to peck like breadcrumbs

SPECIES

There's that which consists
Entirely of an eye
Whose body is the space
Its vision encompasses.

No clue how it got to be that way
As you sit for hours
Spellbound as it were in the midst
Of its deadly eyelashes,

Thinking you need special traps
To catch it, you need
A drop of its mother's milk, a winter evening
Endless and blue.

*

A heart which prowls,
Which rolls over like a stone.
You hear its steps—this heart
Forever receding.

It stole all you had.
You heard its tenderest bones crack
In the maw
Of that moving heart.

You even saw the feathers
Come down one at a time.
Now you only have this mound of spilled salt,
The somber aftertaste of venison.

*

A tongue all alone
In a bird cage
Covered with a blue workshirt
For the night,

Saying not what the leaves are saying,
What the hours, what the wind,
Crimson wind above the haze
Of the streetlights, is saying.

You have to come close and listen.
You have to learn to recognize
The sound of the tongue spreading its wings
Among the weights and measures of the empty cage.

*

Blood too which flows
Like a stream
Through the woods
While you sleep.

You are the line cast
Far and deep in its rushes.
You are the naked hook
Which turns and glitters at its end.

There are no fish,
No rivers, no distant sea to flow into.
Only this bandage unravelling itself
In dizzying hairpin turns.

*

The belly is still earthbound.
Cousin to the rat, it grovels
On crutches—
Parched like an open mouth.

A small mouth
Yet all the world's teeth are in it,
And so are you
Pressed against its cheekbone.

It eats of the earth, it dreams of the earth
Stuck on a spit.
O the earth with an apple in its mouth
At the country fair of the night sky!

*

Where its attendants and keepers,
Late and alone, the instruments
Of torture, the old instruments of subtraction
Undress in the dark

Outside your door, or so it seems
When they enter resplendent with light
Playing along their cutting-edges
Which they offer like sugar-cubes,

Which they offer like a tit
To suck . . . A litter
Huddled in the corner. All your ghostlimbs
Crawling out of their cauls.

TRAVELLING SLAUGHTERHOUSE

Durer, I like that horse of yours.
I spent my childhood hidden in his guts.
The knight looks like my father
The day he came out of prison.

Maria, the redheaded girl goes by
Without giving us a nod. The knight says,
I get up at night to see if the table is still a table.
He says, when I close my eyes everything is so
damn pretty.

We are dawdling in our old backalley.
I see a dog, a goat, but no death.
It must be one of those bleak breezy days
in late autumn.
The horse uses his tail to hold up his pants.

Maria naked in front of a mirror eating an apple.
He says, I love the hair on the nipple to be blonde.
He says, we are a travelling slaughterhouse.
Ah the poor horse, he lets me eat his heart out!

How much death works,
No one knows what a long
Day he puts in. The little
Wife always alone
Ironing death's laundry.
The beautiful daughters
Setting death's supper table.
The neighbors playing
Pinochle in the backyard
Or just sitting on the steps
Drinking beer. Death,
Meanwhile, in a strange
Part of town looking for
Someone with a bad cough,
But the address somehow wrong,
Even death can't figure it out
Among all the locked doors . . .
And the rain beginning to fall.
Long windy night ahead.
Death with not even a newspaper
To cover his head, not even
A dime to call the one pining away,
Undressing slowly, sleepily,
And stretching naked
On death's side of the bed.

A DAY MARKED WITH A SMALL
WHITE STONE

The kindest of all traps
Despite its immaculate steel
And its powerful spring. Bait
Which one inhales like a whiff
Of mint as the breeze changes
Direction.

The languorous, lazy chewing
On the caught leg
Stripped now to the bone. Pain
Joining the silence of trees
And clouds,

In a ring
Of magnanimous coyotes,
In a ring of
Compassionate, melancholy
Something or other . . .

THE HEALER

In a rundown tenement
Under the superhighway,
A healer lives
Who doesn't believe in his power.

An old man with a fat gut,
Hands of a little girl
Which he warms
Over a pan of boiling water.

In his hallway there are
Many wheelchairs, on the stairs
The long howl of the idiot
Led on a leash.

THE CURE

Against seventy-seven kinds of toads
I rubbed myself against in the dark.
Against the rose,
But wholeheartedly for the thorns.
Against windmills. Why the windmills?
Against the angel who's got me pinned down
Like a battering ram. Against all
Grandiose proposals concerning mortality.
Even against that evening
When I held you in my arms.

In abject submission, I offer
The simplicity of this instant,
The Divine Office
Of the empty plate,

Mating season
Of the hand and the glass,
Respectful homage
Of the wine to the light,
Clarity
That I talk to, that I quarrel with . . .

They say of St. John of the Cross
That he would sit,
Just the way I'm sitting now
In a small dark place,
And through a window
Gaze at a distant landscape.

TREES AT NIGHT

Putting out the light
To hear them better

*

To tell the leaves
Of an ash tree
Apart from those
Of a white birch.

*

They would both
Come closer,
They would both whisk me away

*

Images of birds
Fleeing from a fire,
Images of a lifeboat
Caught in the storm.

*

The sound of those
Who sleep without dreams.

*

Being taken hold of
By them.
Being actively taken hold of,
Being carried off
In throes.

*

At times also like the tap
Of a moth
On a windowscreen.

*

A flurry of thoughts.
Sediments
On the bottom of night's ink,
Seething, subsiding.

*

Branches bending
To the boundaries
Of the inaudible.

*

A prolonged hush
That reminds me
To lock the doors.

*

Clarity.
The mast of my spine, for instance,
To which death attaches
A fluttering handkerchief.

*

And the wind makes
A big deal out of it.

ODE

You who are about
to be overlooked

in the heat of, the joy of
the argument

the intangible
I cheat you out of

innocently
and with regret

for such is the spirit
of the law.

*

The mystery of all that is familiar:

the living maze
of the moving fingers

which determines
once and for all

the fall of the dice.

Endless nostalgia
for the concrete

something we could
sink our teeth in

the accompanying
story

of its remarkable properties
to amuse, to astonish

to ease our
suffering.

*

To you who remain
a probability

strict condition
of the invisible

variable
of the imminent

I make these offerings.

*

Because the light
is always with us

and the hush
of an early morning

time propitious
to plain speech

space between the premonition
and the event

the small lovely realm
of the possible.

EUCLID AVENUE

All my dark thoughts
laid out
in a straight line.

An abstract street
on which an equally abstract intelligence
forever advances, doubting
the sound of its own footsteps.

*

Interminable cortege.
Language
as old as rain.
Fortune-teller's spiel

from where it has its beginning,
its kennel and bone
the scent of a stick
I used to retrieve.

*

A sort of darkness without the woods,
crow-light but without the crow,
Hotel Splendide
all locked up for the night.

And out there,
in sight of some ultimate bakery
the street-light
of my insomnia.

*

A place
known as infinity
toward which that old self
advances.

The poor son of poor parents
who aspires to please
at such a late hour.

The magical coins
in his pocket
occupying all his thoughts.

A place known
as infinity,
its screendoor screeching,
endlessly screeching.

THE PRISONER

He is thinking of us.
These leaves, their lazy rustle
That made us sleepy after lunch
So we had to lie down.

He considers my hand on her breast,
Her closed eyelids, her moist lips
Against my forehead, and the shadows of trees
Hovering on the ceiling.

It's been so long. He has trouble
Deciding what else is there.
And all along the suspicion
That we do not exist.

POSITION WITHOUT A MAGNITUDE

As when someone
You haven't noticed before
Gets up in an empty theatre
And projects his shadow
Among the fabulous horsemen
On the screen

And you shudder
As you realize it's only you
On your way
To the blinding sunlight
Of the street.